Praise for

the third part

"I appreciate your to-the-point, accessible, down-to-earth crystallization of the path to Know Thyself."

-Kai Harris, Educator

"This book is a gentle invitation to those who are looking for spiritual connection but are hesitant to take those first steps. Full of insights and free of dogma, Steven shares the deep wisdom he has gained, mostly through honest self-observation, in an easy and accessible style."

-Lila Flood, Musician

"Steven has synthesized timeless wisdom into a very readable book for the layperson ready to investigate their Soul. The essays are intriguing and intelligent. I found myself returning to certain essays because they allowed me to touch into a part of myself I have been longing to connect with. This is like a modern-day Tao Te Ching. Each individual essay is a gem in its own right. Yet to read them together is to go on a journey of self-realization."

-Marie Owl, author of *Planetary Ascension*

the
third
part

our
connection
to **oneness**

Steven Sarsfield

Sacred Dragon Publishing
Los Angeles, California

Sacred Dragon Publishing™
An imprint of Sacred Dragon Publishing Services LLC
Los Angeles, California
SacredDragonPublishing.com

ISBN: 979-8-9876749-1-8 Paperback
ISBN: 979-8-9876749-5-6 Hardcover
ISBN: 979-8-9876749-2-5 eBook

Interior Symbol Art: Steven Sarsfield
Cover and Interior Design: Ryan Forsythe

The information presented in this work is the author's opinion and does not constitute any form of health or medical advice. The content of this work is for informational purposes only and is not intended to diagnose, treat, cure, or prevent any condition or disease or is meant as a substitute for consultation with a licensed practitioner.

Publisher's Cataloging-in-Publication (Provided by Cassidy Cataloguing Services, Inc.).
  Names: Sarsfield, Steven, author.
  Title: The third part : our connection to oneness / Steven Sarsfield.
  Description: Los Angeles, California : Sacred Dragon Publishing, [2024]
  Identifiers: ISBN: 979-8-9876749-1-8 (paperback) | 979-8-9876749-5-6
      (hardcover) | 979-8-9876749-2-5 (ebook)
  Subjects: LCSH: Spiritual life—New Age movement. | Spirituality. |
      Spiritual formation. | Self-realization—Religious aspects. | Wisdom—
      Religious aspects. | Whole and parts (Philosophy) | Holism—
      Religious aspects. | Peace of mind—Religious aspects. | BISAC:
      BODY, MIND & SPIRIT / General. | BODY, MIND & SPIRIT /
      Inspiration & Personal Growth.
  Classification: LCC: BP605.N48 S37 2024 | DDC: 299.93—dc23

Made in the United States of America

*I dedicate this book to my mother,
Maria Christina DeMarco Sarsfield,
and to our maternal lineage for
perseverance and love from time immemorial.*

Author Note

My journey began in Pittsburgh, Pennsylvania, where my Catholic upbringing was shaped by the transformative 60's. After high school, I served in the military and later found myself in California, immersed in the trucking industry. It was during this time that I felt a pull towards Buddhism, Astrology, Zen, and other esoteric studies, marking a significant shift in my spiritual path.

From there, I started a couple of moderately successful businesses. But as my life began to revolve around raising my children, I realized that a more stable income was necessary, and after some schooling, I began a 30-year-long career as a Land Surveyor.

My life has blossomed from a time of internal struggles to receiving and appreciating the gifts of the universe. While working in different fields and having my own businesses, I witnessed the day-to-day demands of the emotional lives of many of my friends and associates. Together with a lifelong inquiry into the spiritual side of life, I saw the need for a modern retelling of the wisdom of the ages.

For eight years, I kept this book alive in my heart. It is based on a life of thoughtfulness and wonder that has distilled my experiences and learning into an accessible portrayal of the inner life.

This book is a teaching, but it is more than a lecture or information. It is a recognition of the landscape of our being. When this truth resonates within, the resulting peace of being recognized as yourself brings not only the relaxation of struggle but also a clear path forward.

Contents

Introduction

In ancient times, the spiritual part of life was abundant. The world's great religions were seeded by the spiritual deeds of that time. In the past 1,000 years or so, however, many religious institutions shifted away from spiritual wisdom toward unwavering dogma. The vestiges of older spiritual ways, now locked away in monasteries, secret societies, and indigenous lineages, are barely intact.

We are now in a time when much of humanity is either rejecting or clinging to religious dogma. For some, religion, as practiced today, has been bled dry of spiritual meaning by greed and politics. Others hold onto their beliefs to the exclusion of any alternative. How can this book help?

Those who cling with hope to historic narratives shrouded in mystery, diluted by time, and transformed by special interests can learn to use their steadfast willpower to allow universal truths to guide them. Those who have been disillusioned by obscure references, priestly decadence, and otherworldly hypotheses can find the peace they long for in the refuge of their own inner wisdom. And many who don't believe in the doctrines they've been exposed to can start to believe in their own divine nature.

We can all open to the eternal spirit everyone shares and, as a result, see the truth of non-separation in each other. As a united people of Earth, we will stop the wars and heal the sick. *The Third Part* offers a small push down a long road for a humanity destined for enlightenment.

This collection of short essays is intended for you to have a better relationship with your true self, not by following some prescribed dogma but by uncovering your deepest motivations. The process described in these essays led me to an inconceivably different life than I had ever imagined.

I present this book because I believe our media and our culture support the idea that, as human beings, we are primarily a body and a mind. I am certain everyone believes there is another part of our being—a Third Part. Every day, in each waking hour, we are subjected to messages that see us only as a two-part being—physical and mental. This brainwashing has seeped into our deepest motivations. Many are confused, disillusioned, or distracted. As a counterbalance to this two-part perception of humans, this book is a cheerleader for the Third Part of our being—the spiritual self, the Soul, the True Self—to move us toward experiencing the wholeness of our divine nature.

I don't believe the Third Part within us is far away or difficult to find. I believe it is always present and active. We just don't recognize it because we've not been taught how to do that. People ask, "How can I tell if the voice inside my head is a message from my Third Part or mere fantasy?" I hope that something in this book will help you answer that question with certainty.

There are many dissatisfied people on this planet, and the consciousness of our culture reflects that. While our physical and mental evolution has affected this consciousness, our intentions, beliefs, thoughts, and actions substantially impact world affairs and foster or lessen our dissatisfaction with it. As more individuals on this planet find the truth inside themselves, new opportunities for solving our world's problems will emerge from this more awake and aware human collective. It's up to you, me, and everyone to bring about positive change in the world, in every moment, through our thoughts, beliefs, and actions that are aligned with the Third Part.

The power of this spiritual awakening is not reaching a larger audience who find themselves put off by mysticism and some of the New Age jargon. My intention is to bridge that divide and awaken the connection with the Third Part in simple and practical ways.

I am an elder. My life has been full and rewarding. I have also made a lot of mistakes. I used those same mistakes to provide a viewing platform from which to examine my motives. My parents were children of poor, hard-working immigrants. They grew up during the Great Depression, never having enough. I was raised to live frugally and work hard. Somehow, this evolved into me becoming a selfish person. The idea that there would never be enough and what I did have could be easily lost made me very protective of what I had earned. Survival was the paramount focus of my early life. I felt it was my responsibility to be self-sufficient in a world of competition. I lived this way for years. I was not rich, not even always employed.

I did not care about others' hardships and rarely shared my knowledge or skills without considering what was in it for me. I used people. I was scared. My world was populated with competitors. It was terribly lonely. Punctuated by illusions of success, I wallowed in my fear of losing that which I never possessed: the ability to direct my life.

Then, something changed. I noticed that I was criticizing others for their selfish behavior and realized my hypocrisy. At first, I didn't want to consider that I could be viewed this way by people, but slowly, I accepted the truth of my selfishness and the need for change. My habits were strong, and the imprints of my youth formed a solid foundation for my self-identity. I did, however, have a persistent recognition that I was missing out on finer points in life. For everyone, there comes a time when dissatisfaction with life's path is so great and despair of supposed effectiveness so overwhelms us, that we are forced to search for a new direction.

With each collapse of some unfounded anticipation of loss, I wondered what logic lay beneath the fear of loss. I began to see how fear controlled my thoughts and actions. I paid close attention to the outcomes of my decisions. I took the long view and asked myself how choices made long ago slowly unfolded, affecting my life experiences years later. I accepted the responsibility for my choices, although, at times, I had to swallow hard as I took stock of the results and was easily drawn into thinking of myself as less than worthy.

When I looked deeper at this evolving picture of my life, I began to see how little my constant search for something more or better actually paid off. Although there were positive outcomes in that picture, most of them were the result of something unplanned or unexpected. Gradually, I learned to accept full responsibility for all my decisions and realized how powerful I was in creating my life experiences. I just had to learn how to use that power in a better way.

I started to read everything I could find on conscious awakening, including books by Eastern mystics and Western philosophers. I became ever more eager to change when I realized how much I had missed by living my closed-down, only-me life. Still, I was not in the best economic shape, and the challenge of daily survival was a constant contrast to my expanding awareness.

Encouraged by these spiritual messages, my self-acceptance grew. I found that I was less worried about the future. I began to understand my own impermanence as a physical being. I approached life with a more giving attitude that brought me a resilience I had never experienced before. Something inside felt calmer, and this ease of being gave me the perseverance to keep going. Through studying many teachings and philosophies, keeping what spoke to me, and setting aside the rest, I came to understand that I had not made wise choices. I was afraid, uninformed, shortsighted, or lazy. I used my willpower inappropriately.

One way of looking at how I was changed by my expanding awareness is that my luck changed. Another view is that in the process of self-reflection and expansion, I shifted from only looking at what I could get out of life to noticing the world around me and seeing it in a whole new way. The stillness and eternal makeup of the natural world seduced me into believing in my higher powers. Again and again, I would encounter some wild part of the world with awe and wonder: beaches, mountains, forests, rocks, sunsets, and oceans. What part of me was appreciating this beauty, I asked myself. I could not deny that the unrestrained beauty and magnificence were also in me. Gradually, the realization came—I am a part of everything; we all are.

After that, opportunities for rewarding employment and close friendships appeared. I met people who told me they thought I was a good person, giving me confidence for more ease in my life. I found myself encouraging others, improving my relationships, and looking deeper into the choices I made. I stopped believing in my fear. If I failed at something, it was a lesson. I replaced anticipation with wonder. Life went on. No, fear is not gone. And I often struggle with it anew. But the fear is not in control anymore. I have shed that burden.

Many people I meet are suffering silently and alone as I had. If I can inspire someone to shift from relying on outcomes to seeking to be a more whole person, this shift brings us together to change the world. The world changes because individuals like you and me have the courage to look within to create transformation; like casting a stone into water, our example sends ripples of integrity throughout the world.

I intend only to provide motivation for you to acknowledge the Third Part of your being. I am not going to try to explain it to you because there are no rational explanations for it. Your association with this Third Part, in every way that you connect with it, is not like anyone else's. Your experience will not be like mine. The way you notice its influence will belong to you. You will not be able to describe it. It's okay. You are unique. That's the complexity of Earth. There are close to eight billion of us, and no two are the same. That is why this path involves only you.

My practice is this: I believe I am more than a body and a mind. I continue to remove unsubstantiated beliefs from my life and become balanced in body, mind, and Third Part. I'm not asking you to do what I do or even learn from what I did. I am not trying to persuade you. You will either identify with these concepts or not.

If we were friends and you actually felt *seen* by me, that might make you feel pretty good. If your closest relations could see the real you, that would even feel better. But nothing will prepare you for the joy of being seen as who you really are when you see yourself through the eyes of the Third Part. It will be like finding a best friend, who sometimes must tell you things that seem difficult to hear and sometimes offers you a gift that resonates with a need you didn't even remember you had.

I hope to remind you in as many ways as I can that there is more to your being than what you do and what you think. I will tell you what I know. I will be the cheering section, encouraging you to practice living in harmony with the Third Part.

Whether you read this from front to back or let your intuition guide you to the perfect page, keep it close by, like a friend you can call on anytime. There will come times when what you need is just some motivation. Try to examine the source of your feelings, take a breath, and open to a page. See if the words address how you feel. Close the book. Do you notice ease or reluctance coming up? Every effort you make toward understanding your true feelings and motivations will be rewarded.

1

BEGINNINGS

It doesn't matter what you believe in;
it matters how often you act on those beliefs.

The philosophy of this book is based on two ideas: enlightenment is not that far away, and it's only our resistance to change that keeps us from it.

There are many books and practices to aid the pursuit of bettering one's life. But while a specific practice or belief can provide instruction, the motivation and perseverance for betterment must come from within.

The promise of an eternal reward for following a belief system is a sufficient motivation for some. But for others, the confusion of the belief systems' commands and rituals, coupled with its departure from one's daily trials, leads to half-hearted observance and may result in the complete denial of any extraordinary life at all.

Whatever path you are on for connecting with inner knowing, my objective is to motivate you to pursue your best self amid the trials of daily life by offering calmness, support, recognition, and a bit of wisdom. But mostly, I want to inspire a belief in your innate ability to progress on the path to enlightenment, even when you don't notice that you're making progress.

The moment-by-moment daily interactions of life are where your practice and your beliefs matter. Inner peace will arrive when you are spontaneously guided by your beliefs instead of trying to live up to them. This is a different kind of belief.

It's not about believing who you're supposed to be; it's about believing who you really are.

Can you make the mystery of life stronger
in you than habit or false security?

The purpose of this book is to restate Universal Truths acceptable to readers who have a healthy suspicion of dogma.

In many religions, there are ancient books to study and famous persons to emulate. The historical attire, repetitive motions, and reverential language have come to overshadow the original spiritual doctrines.

Dogma relieves the challenge of personal examination for many, and most of us have relied on some parts of dogmatic teachings in our lives. An undying faith in what history, saints, and long-lasting religions teach can give some a foothold on their sanity. And I acknowledge that untying from established formula and stepping into an unknown world is daunting.

My suggestion, therefore, is that rather than having faith in following another's path, one allows the lighthearted openness for a personalized approach of accepting the mystery that there are things in the Universe and within us that are yet to be discovered.

In this way, we gain knowledge of ourselves. Gaining knowledge isn't always about facts. Often, it is more about the experience than about gaining content.

Everybody has a different path.

Another reason I don't favor religious dogma is the assumption that there is a single path to enlightenment or heaven or whatever. I ask myself how a single system could be perfect for everybody.

But where does one start an examination of self that questions the validity of historic, religious-based dogma? Perhaps we can look at what's deep inside each and every one of us right now. While that past is interesting and has some value in providing historical context, our life occurs in the present moment. We are living now, not in the past.

There are many lessons we each need to learn. And we're not all on the same lesson plan. Reliance on dogma cannot solve all the answers to billions of individual lesson plans and each person's individual issues.

Once we accept the nature of our path, we can begin to see others' struggles as different from ours in content only. Struggle is a common element in everyone's life.

Believing that the other person is wrong because they may not have learned a lesson that you have learned is referred to as a lack of compassion. Stop it.

Body, Mind, and Soul

I have studied many religions and esoteric sciences. I can find only one idea on which they all agree: We are beings with a corporal body, a mind, and what I call the Third Part. Some refer to this part as spirit, soul, or higher self. The descriptions do not matter. We all know it exists.

In common Western usage, we are familiar with the terms body, mind, and spirit. Some say body, mind, and soul. There may be other words one chooses. In this book, I ask the reader to allow me to use words that may not have a universally agreed upon definition, like Soul or spirit, but convey a general understanding or thought that is useful for conceptualizing an idea or suggestion.

The Kabbalists call the three parts mineral, vegetable, and animal. The Rosicrucians see the Soul as different from the spirit. Buddhists, Hindus, and indigenous peoples have their own words. I feel it is more worthwhile to wonder what this part of my being is rather than name it properly.

I am going to use body, mind, and Soul as the names for three distinct parts of our sense of being because of their general acceptance. I also will use the Third Part to refer to the Soul because the phrase lacks any predetermined meaning.

Living without access to the Third Part is like being in a three-piece music ensemble, and only two members show up for the performance. The music is much more rich, full, and complete when all three performers and instruments are engaged and playing together in harmony.

My use of the word Soul does not suggest that I subscribe to or agree with its meaning or usage in religious texts, and I invite you also to absolve yourself from your own preconceived ideas about its meaning. We shall see that it is up to each of us to make a personal discovery of our Third Part. Name it whatever you want.

Balancing our Three Parts

What does it mean to balance our three parts? First of all, balance does not mean equal. Balance has more to do with harmony, and harmony means the ability to adjust to circumstances.

There are times when we are out of balance by having a preoccupation with the body or mind, physical or mental aspects of our being. Sometimes, engaging only with these aspects of ourselves is so habitual that the Third Part, the Soul, is not even recognized, noticed, or given a small part of daily energy.

This attraction to the physical experience is understandable; the physical world is very alluring. We can either use our food, clothing, and possessions for their intended purpose or view them as our personalities. You know these people. You may be one yourself: always talking about what they have, what they are going to get, how much better, shinier, and more expensive their thing is. Who would we be without our things?

It's the same with the attraction to mental aspects of life that can get blown out of proportion by an over-reliance or identity based on what we think we know, what we've read, or what scholastic accolades we have received.

It takes considerable courage to refine our body and mind's control of our being. We use these aspects to receive recognition and approval, which we so desperately require when the Third Part is not the sustaining feature of our lives.

I am not suggesting the abandonment of the physical or mental. Balance for most is bringing the Third Part out of seclusion and having its energy complement the others.

There is an eternal part in us right now.

There is this eternal energy that we all possess, and it's free. It will always be within and offer guidance whenever we let it. It is with us every minute. Just like we can strengthen the body or mind, we can also strengthen access to this eternal part.

When we are caught up in the noise and distraction of the external world, it's very hard to hear and connect with the inner world of our Third Part, our Soul. At this point, living life without having access to and hearing my Soul's guidance would be like traveling without a map. I have found numerous benefits in accessing my Soul's guidance, not least of which is peace of mind. Can you envision all three parts of your being acting together?

The main theme of this book is how the simple act of changing how we see ourselves can have a surprising effect and impact on our lives.

The Third Part is the eternal part you know is there. Paying more attention to the idea that each one of us is body, mind, and Third Part can lead to a more balanced life.

I am not an enlightened being.

There is no guarantee that we will reach complete enlightenment before our present bodies die.

But we have a choice in how we spend our time and energy in this life, getting closer to the truth on our path to enlightenment.

We need constant awareness, reminding ourselves of our fictionalization of the concept of enlightenment, being open to a new understanding, and welcoming of its potential.

Many are seeking enlightenment as a path to comfort or pleasure. The search for completion is not the same as the search for satisfaction. Completion is the culmination of our spiritual endowment. Satisfaction is a temporary belief that the mind is content.

I am not running away from my existence to a better place with better things. I believe a certain amount of discontent sustains the practice of awareness, which, along with a certainty that there is more to life than the worldly culture promises, brings the discernment necessary for growth.

Putting Together the Puzzle

I encourage a healthy sense of both curiosity and questioning when considering my views or any other philosophical perspective. In that open-minded inquiry, perhaps scavenging for some redeemable pieces of advice strikes the right balance. For example, this book is not offered as the answer to everything or anything that does not satisfy your own sense of truth. I am not here to tell you what to do or think; just passing along some things that have worked for me that may, in small or big ways, work for you too.

Perhaps a helpful analogy to bring this point home is how one might approach piecing together a jigsaw puzzle. Suppose you have never done a jigsaw puzzle and asked me how to do it. I would tell you to find all the pieces with a straight edge and construct the puzzle's border. I like this approach because it's very rewarding for not a whole lot of work.

Next, I might encourage you to put like colors in the same place to make it a little easier to find the right colored pieces for a blue sky or yellow flowers, for instance.

Now, mind you, I haven't seen your puzzle, either the box top picture or the pieces. I'm not going to be able to put any of it together for you. You are on your own. Just as I can't put your puzzle together, I can only offer suggestions about how to proceed on your path. I can't know the struggles in your life, but I can offer suggestions that work for me.

The analogy of life being a puzzle is an interesting one—not valid in all circumstances, for sure, but somewhat illuminating.

In our lives, we look at our experiences and try to fit the ones that seem to belong together. Failure after failure co-mingled with intermittent and joyful successes. We keep trying because we trust that all the pieces will eventually come together. We know this will work out.

Each failure to find some corresponding meaning in life is just an opportunity to see if two other pieces are going to come together.

Expect frustration. Expect fulfillment.

**Let the ideas in this book remind you
of the sacred truths you hold within.**

I am not trying to convince you of every one of my beliefs. You will notice a resonance when an idea or belief settles softly within. Also, be aware of those ideas that seem startling or create some inner turmoil. These may be areas of your consciousness that are ripe for examination.

We can't know sacred truths in our minds with logic. Nor can we pass them from one to another with words. Our deepest parts are not logical. This is what makes life frustrating for some. The need for understanding is overwhelming and, at the same time, not always rewarding.

How will you know if an idea presented in this book resembles the truth? Life truly is a mystery to the mind. But you are more than mind, and this book invites you to welcome and explore your other part. Giving substantial acknowledgment to these places within you can reinforce acceptance of core beliefs.

We are all connected to Oneness. Our access to truth is identical. This book is meant to remind you of what you already hold inside.

I don't believe in the God you don't believe in.

In this book, I will use the word God.

If I had to pick a word that described a belief in some ultimate existence, it would be *truth*. I do believe that there is an ultimate truth.

Realizing my ineffectiveness in reaching an accurate conclusion about the nature of God is actually a relief. I quit trying to decide what God is or isn't.

The path I am on compels me to focus on other things.

On this path, I expect to grow, to reinterpret. I expect that my relationship with many of my current opinions may undergo major changes. For example, the relationship I have, or a belief I have in a higher being, is bound to evolve.

Most importantly, my philosophy does not require there be an ultimate divinity, just the recognition of the possibility of Oneness.

You cannot avoid enlightenment.

Proponents of a steadfast pursuit of a spiritual life make a good point: consistently reaching, trying, and learning will undoubtedly provide some advancement. This book, however, proposes that even without such purposeful and consistent direction, the core nature of our being is propelling us toward enlightenment.

Our evolution toward enlightenment isn't about being weak or strong, committed or not committed, or following special rules. It's an inevitability. With all due respect to Darwin's theory of "survival of the fittest" as the principal trajectory of evolution, I believe the human species is evolving through *spiritual selection.* Evidence points to the growth of consciousness in our species.

This is not about who finds the food but who notices and engages with shifts in our collective consciousness.

The truth is inevitable. All words are lies.

Perhaps this is startling to read, but it needs to be stated. These words we use and the logic we use them with are insufficient to explain the nature of the Universe or our place in it.

Nothing I say in this book is the truth.

What will come to pass as the truth will never depend on what you or I think or say. It would be presumptuous to think that we can define or predict the Universal reality in our present physically dependent state.

We try our best to use thought patterns, turn them into words, and convey meaning. Our words are allegories, metaphors, stories, or parables. I believe there are allegories to truth in the collective human consciousness. These old sayings have no owners, no originating myth, and no proponents. Yet, they last for centuries. I'm convinced that their longevity belies truth and meaning. One of my favorites is "God works in mysterious ways." How can we interpret this in a modern way?

In math, a placeholder is used when there is a variable or an unknown. In this book, words are used as placeholders. Let's agree we don't yet have a unified definition for some of these words.

The value of the placeholder is derived at the end of the computation. Some words as placeholders used in this book may not reveal their meaning until the end of the book or even later.

2

FOUNDATIONS

Soul Variations

When we look at human bodies, we see variations in shapes and sizes, abilities, and health. Creation's splendor relies on multiple possibilities.

In the vastness of the world, the expressions of the mind's ability to think and create vary greatly. Consider the great thinkers and artists of the world, such as Pythagoras, DaVinci, and Einstein, at one extreme, and those with cognitive impairment at the other and every other expression in between.

How can it be that our Souls' experiences are not similarly differentiated with an infinite array of possibilities?

My understanding suggests that each Soul is just as unique as the individual expressions of body and mind.

Reincarnation. Enlightenment. Oneness.

I invite you to consider these three concepts with an open mind. I cannot prove to you what they represent; however, I rely on them as the basis for my belief of existence. Throughout this book, these concepts will be expanded on. Here is a brief explanation to begin the journey.

Reincarnation

The way I look at reincarnation is that it is a more reasonable explanation of the stages of Soul growth than others I have encountered—not that reasonableness is the only test for determining the truthfulness of such esoteric concepts, but it's a good starting point that helps me sift through the competing ideas.

The scientific research examining those who are born with very accurate memories of past lives suggests there is some proof of beings progressing through many lives.

I was brought up to believe my Soul was created in 1948 and that it will live forever. I was told this Soul has an eternal future but no past life. To me, that is not reasonable; nothing in the Universe works this way.

I can't describe what part of me is eternal, but I believe we have been born before and will be born again.

Enlightenment
We are beings of indescribable origin and evolution. Our enlightenment cannot be avoided.

I am not a completely enlightened being. I dare say you are not either. I don't expect either of us to be completely enlightened in this lifetime. While possible, I think it might take a bit longer than that.

Enlightenment, to me, is the settling of the discord between my perceived manifestation and my true nature.

Oneness
Oneness means that we are all connected, not that we are all the same. Each of us has uniqueness as well as similarity.

I believe that the entire Universe is connected in a unified field of energy. Everything exists and communicates as a vibrational frequency. Oneness is completeness, which means that you and I, and everyone and everything, are a part of this Oneness.

Belief in Oneness is the first step towards recognizing access to this unified field.

Recognizing the already existing connection with Oneness.

Can we suspend, for a moment, the insistence that our physical bodies and busy minds are all we are?

Many believe that the creativity and the synchronicity of Oneness are present in their lives at one time or another. Through self-exploration and reflection, we have an opportunity to look deep inside ourselves and imagine that there could be another part of our being, a part we could and should get to know better.

Can we believe that what is happening to us at any moment is exactly what is supposed to be happening?

Longing Is. The Soul powers the longing.

How much of who we are can we attribute to the Soul's eternal longing for Oneness?

Every day, in ways we may not immediately recognize, we move along the path toward enlightenment. Each of us progresses at a pace that is most suitable to our level of consciousness.

Moreover, that progress is always underway. And to each one in a different way.

I call this drive toward fulfilling the Soul's desire to realize and experience Oneness a longing. Although it changes with intensity, this longing is always present.

When I reach for it, it doesn't always provide an answer, but the feeling of the constant reliability of its presence provides me the calmness with which to proceed.

One cannot know enlightenment;
one can only be enlightenment.

Here's some truth. No one can describe what enlightenment is. Not the clergy, monks, or shamans. Words are never going to be able to describe a state of consciousness. Wanting to know or realize the True Self and enlightenment is not the same as having already decided what this means or how to get there.

Being open to what enlightenment might be is a key point of my philosophical exploration in this book. To me, the only piece of honest information we have to guide us on our journey is that we don't know exactly what the goal is.

We will be enlightened when we get there by the absence of the longing.

We are not who we were.

Everything that we have done has been by our inherent power. We are responsible for every mess we have ever been in and for every joy we have ever felt. Regret is merely a distraction from the present moment.

We may look at our past and believe that a wrong has been done and that a different decision could, or should, have been made. But by whom? The person we are today is not the person who made that decision. Why judge our past decisions by our present beliefs?

We are not guilty of wrongdoing. We may have been proceeding with false information in instances that appear to our present mind as wrong. We did what we did, and now we have that experience. It was a lesson. Our consciousness expanded.

If we accept our and others' imperfections in this life and see all actions as lessons we are learning, it is possible to reconcile the past with grace and live without shame or blame.

3

DISPELLING MYTHS

Umbrellas in the sand.
You do not have to search for Oneness.

This is a metaphor. I am at the beach on a sunny day. I am surrounded by umbrellas that are blocking out all but a few shafts of sunlight.

Above the canopy of shade, however, the sun is shining brightly.

The umbrellas are like the illusions in my mind that block the light of Oneness from shining in my life. In the Third Part, the gift of eternal Truth shines bright. One by one, I begin to close each umbrella by discovering which unsubstantiated beliefs I am holding on to that keep the illusion in place.

As each umbrella closes, dispelling another illusion, the light of Oneness shines upon my life and all I see, illuminating acceptance and understanding.

Noticing the Small Changes in Consciousness

The reluctance to be patient is birthed in the fear that we are not enough. Driven by ambition, we believe that a significant change in consciousness is necessary for spiritual progress. However, spiritual progress may occur in unnoticed and seemingly insignificant ways.

We tend to think that patience means standing still and doing nothing. But patience gives us the space to notice clarity, creativity, and opportunity.

Our desire to become greater in the future is not the same as the desire to see things differently in each present moment.

With patience, we utilize our ability to recognize the countless opportunities and offerings Oneness affords us.

It's not possible to think outside the box.

The mind is the box.

The mind believes that the mind can figure a way out of a box it has created. It excels in habitual behavior, and its job is not to locate a new idea.

As children, we seek stability, and our first disappointments are the unreliability of this earthly existence. We are trained to find comfort in the familiar and disregard the unfamiliar. The mind's constant interjecting of what will happen next keeps us in the box.

There is wondering outside the box.

Wondering is the courage to function without a preconceived outcome. Imagination is a gift of the Third Part. Wondering is how we open that gift.

When our lives are based on the wonder of now, the things that come into our lives have meaning. The Divine center in us must work not by determining reality but by coinciding with it.

The Fundamental Contradiction

The mind causes the suffering that it seeks to eliminate. The mind cannot be both the problem and the solution.

There is a fundamental contradiction in our refusal to understand that our mind imposes the very experience of suffering that it seeks to dispel.

Invalid assumptions of the mental process that view the cause of suffering as something outside of our mind are the actual cause of our perceived suffering.

Our self-protective rational mind operates under a cover of persuasion and misrepresentation. It uses these manipulations to avoid the resolution of the inner conflict and to remain indispensable for our well-being.

What is one to use as motivation?

There is a time when one must be motivated solely by belief. The doubts of the mind must be allowed to rise without consequence.

Occasionally, one encounters brief successes. These successes invigorate and build courage. After this, motivation can be shifted from belief to certainty. Of course, motivation is just the beginning. Our certainty will surely be tested.

Spiritualists often speak of "being on the path." But perhaps before we can presume to be on a spiritual path, there are uncertainties of life to navigate that are full of thickets, deadfall, and underbrush obstructing our view and promising sidetracks leading nowhere. I call this the track. By contrast, the path is open and well-trod but rife with delusion and distraction.

The track for me was without success, trying one thing after another, looking for repeatable consequences to try to unravel my motivations. Trying and failing, trying and failing.

I decided to forgo my idea that I could find my way forward. I had to give up the delusion of my knowledge.

I had to admit that I was making choices based on fear. I was merely avoiding what I perceived as a danger to my ego. Slowly, I became able to keep going in one direction and not be intimidated by fear or attracted by quick results.

Then I came to the path. This was, for me, a belief in my inherent worthiness. I felt like I was being moved along by a force that was not entirely within me but, at the same time, was not external. The path doesn't provide a goal.

There was almost as much chaos but less struggle.

All love songs are prayers.

Think of the words of any love song. *I want you. I miss you. I want you back. Please come into my life. You are everything to me. I'm sorry. We'll be so happy together.*

All songs and poems, even thoughts for that matter, about love are love statements to and from our higher selves. Prayers.

When we sing along to the basic Universal intelligence of a love song, our hearts are longing for that ultimate lover, the God within.

4

ACKNOWLEDGING AND ACCEPTING EMOTIONS

Feelings are not Emotions;
Emotions are not Feelings.

I find that most of us use these words interchangeably. They are not the same.

In the realm of body, mind, and Third Part, feelings are the messaging from the body to the mind, and emotions are the messaging from the Soul to the mind.

Although this is an important distinction as we travel the path to self-discovery, emotions, and feelings have one important similarity—neither communicate through the spoken word.

When the body *speaks* to us, it is not with words. When we are hungry, or cold, or hurt, there is a message that reaches the mind through the nerves brought about by a biochemical interaction. The mind translates these feelings into the words, "I am hungry." From birth, we were trained by our caregivers to translate the feeling of hungry into words: "Is baby hungry?"

Our caregivers, however, rarely trained us on how to translate emotional messages. "Does baby feel neglected because mommy is doing other things?" "Is baby confused because daddy is inconsistent?"

One way our Third Part speaks to us is through the inner voice of our emotions. Some refer to this as the silent voice. It is to our benefit to be aware of this messaging of emotions and to consider the often misinterpreted meaning we give to them.

Whether we receive these emotions with joy or annoyance, they are provided as guides to deeper beliefs we often overlook.

Where do our emotions come from?

Emotions do not belong to us. They are Universal energies with which we can resonate at any given time. These energies exist outside of us, everywhere, always. The triggers we have developed instantly go to that resonance like an auto-tune button on the radio. We find ourselves in these emotional cages but never see ourselves going in the trap door.

Many have tried various methods to free themselves from unwanted emotions. Most are not successful for two reasons.

One is the belief that if we can somehow gain control over our minds, we will be able to guide ourselves to the emotional outcome we desire. Not only does this never work, but it causes us to hide our true emotions. We need to access these emotions and not cover them up with false serenity.

The other method is to force preferred or pleasant emotions to be stronger than unpleasant ones—such as having fun or compulsive addictions.

This assumes that we can stay in a constant state of happiness, and these unwanted emotions will never have a chance to compete. This is escapism, but there is nowhere to escape. Many travel these dead-ends, some for a lifetime.

Sooner or later, the time comes when we don't have the strength to push emotions away or have another escape mechanism in place. This is pain.

We cannot change our emotions.

Emotions are not under the control of the will. None of us will always feel love or never get angry again.

The perpetual state of not accepting the emotional landscape of our lives can lead to a feeling of helplessness, which is perhaps the source of much anguish in the world.

Confronting what is going on inside of us is our responsibility. Though we cannot change emotions, we can become more adept at recognizing the underlying causes of our emotional state, exposing what our mind has hidden from us.

71

Being Accurate

We can't be accurate about the future; we can only be accurate about the present moment.

When I was younger, I drove a big rig truck. I spent a lot of time listening to the Universe, harmonizing with the vibrations I felt around me. I often drove all night and could feel the dawn coming—alarm clocks ringing, coffee pots sputtering, showers steaming. The daily buzz of humanity would grow louder and faster as the sun rose.

Occasionally, I was late getting out of the shipping terminal. I had to be at the delivery address in five hours, but it was a seven-hour drive. It was possible for me to drive the whole way, considering my late arrival. But upon reflection, I realized that no one at the destination was even up or had any idea where I was. At the destination dock, it was just another lonely, chilly night.

When I searched for lateness, it was in the future, not the present. In the present moment, I was not late. I had made it up. I could, instead, have five hours of peace.

Of course, there came that ominous moment in time when the dockworker looked out the open door, saw nothing, and glanced at his watch. Yup, then I was late. OK, so I pulled into the truck stop, called in to report my status, got back in the cab, and peacefully continued on my way.

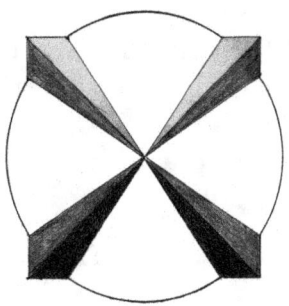

If there is something hidden in me, I want to find it.

For all of us, we have times when the world seems to be on our side. Our energies are strong, decisions come easily, and we feel loved and appreciated. If this is how you feel all the time, throw this book away and, please, write your own.

But except for a rare few, we also have times when it seems like life has taken a bit of a left turn. I experience that when I feel helpless about a situation or stuck in a persistent emotion. Sometimes, I just feel like I can't figure out what to do next.

That's when I know I need to reconcile my true emotions. Something has triggered me, but I'm not sure what it is. Sometimes, rather than focus my attention on trying to discern the cause of the emotion, I surrender to the passion of immersing in the emotion to see what appears from the depths of the experience.

I don't necessarily believe in evil. However, I try to notice a difference between being guided by energies with comfort and peace and being misled by unsubstantiated beliefs.

How true is what we perceive?

Most of us have a phone with a camera. The camera lens is always open to receive light, but we choose what light images to capture and place on the phone's screen. In a similar way, we get to choose what life images we capture and place on the screen of our perception. We make choices about the visual stimulation recorded on our inner screen whenever we focus our attention, stare, or daydream.

This ability to choose what gets noticed, identified, and recognized is a very powerful ability and has a profound effect on who we think we are. It is a reflection of what we believe we perceive.

Do the images on the screen of your perception reflect threat-assessment surveillance based in fear? Are there images of love and understanding? What else is there? What do you want to see there?

Either move forward with audacity and strength or wait. It's delusional to think the suffering mind knows what to do next.

You've heard the story of the drowned man at heaven's gate, asking why, since he was a *God-fearin' man,* he wasn't saved from a flood by God. And God tells him, "I sent you a warning, then a boat, then a helicopter. You turned them away and said you were waiting for God."

Miracles are not always what we perceive them to be.

I ask myself how many metaphorical boats and helicopters offering passage to my higher self have I turned down because I was looking elsewhere for an illuminated path to enlightenment.

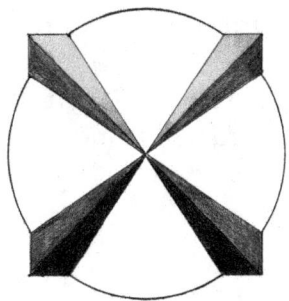

Ego is a tool. When not needed, it will diminish in importance.

There is a lot of discussion about the ego. Not many have agreed on what the heck that is. But there are a lot of folks who say we need to get rid of it.

I have a different view. We don't get very far in life without taking intentional action. So, there must be some energy within us that drives us to action, strives for life. Sometimes, we need it to be protective or combative. Other times, we might need it to be wily or even playful.

In my view, ego is this tool. But like any tool, it works best if used for the purpose it was designed for, then stored properly when not in use.

We need the ego's help when the going gets rough. It needs to be in the driver's seat to safely navigate us through many of life's daily challenges. When the claims on our attention by the frivolous distractions of the world get louder, we need ego's courage and strength.

When we feel the warmth of eternal peace, we put the ego away for a while. Eventually, we realize it's not needed anymore.

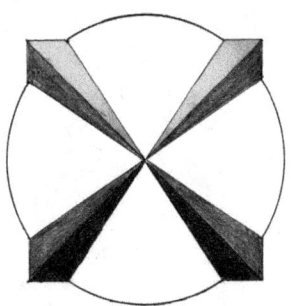

We are neither as good nor as bad
as we sometimes think we are.

Our unrecognized fears are more of a problem than any action we have done.

The Third Part is waiting to help uncover these hidden fears and remove them from our path toward enlightenment.

Minimizing the desire for distractions allows the Third Part to be a more active partner in moving us through our pain and life lessons quickly and with greater ease.

We don't have to forgive ourselves, or anyone, for any past mistakes because neither we nor they have committed any. At worst, we made decisions with unfortunate or harmful consequences based on confusion and illusion. We all experiment and grow with each result.

Eventually, we may find that our desire for truth far outweighs our desire for distractions.

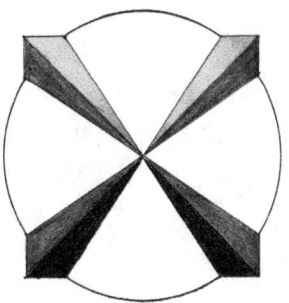

We have all had and given pain.

The reason that we tend to become condescending at another's mistakes is that we emotionally resonate with how they feel. We have been there and done that. When we witness others submerge in their pain, we feel that pain. When we witness cruelty, it can stir a memory of our own cruelty, reminding us that we were once convinced of the necessity of violence.

Some of us may think we have demons. But mostly, these are memories of past lives when we allowed fear, intolerance, and separation to ensure our survival.

History is replete with enormous human suffering from war, disease, starvation, and persecution. All of us, in past lives, experienced these traumas. We have also been the cause of trauma in others. Then, the justification for torture and even murder seemed reasonable.

For many, the reasonableness of violence has given way to the understanding of its inadequacy. Of the many reasons that we justified putting ourselves first, none provided the desired outcome we thought it would.

But immature Souls coming into manifestation on this planet believe in the need for self-protection at the expense of another's suffering. We react in horror as we witness others struggling with this kind of existence. We have all gone through these same terrifying and often violent life lessons.

If we are able to live a life of peace and prosperity, it is because we have experienced the truth of our past actions over lifetimes. We understand our past failures in promoting our expectations through violence.

As we become less guilty and ashamed of our past, it has less power to persuade our current decisions. We begin to make choices that forego the temptation of separation and move toward wholeness and Oneness.

Acknowledge emotions.
Stop blaming; start feeling.

A basic step of becoming enlightened is a continuous practice of accurately determining and acknowledging emotions.

The difficulty of this approach is the mind's habit of distracting us from the true emotion and confusing it with blame. Many of our fear-based emotions, like abandonment or injustice, are too painful to admit. Blame is much less self-threatening. We miss out on so many opportunities for self-examination while we are focusing on the mistakes of others.

Don't confuse admitting we have anger with the idea of not getting angry. Stopping emotional responses is not possible, and suppressing awareness of unfavorable emotions is the source of many Soul problems. We cannot control how or when an emotional reaction of anger is triggered. But we do have a choice to dwell in that anger or not.

We all have experienced anger while driving. The usual response to a perceived infraction and its accompanying irritability is to consider the guilt and fault of the other. Wishing evil is not uncommon. The ensuing moments of self-righteousness are a distraction that we seem to prefer over contemplating our true emotions.

All perceived injustices are perfect opportunities for self-evaluation. Is someone making you late? What are the results of being late? What feels threatened? Did someone not follow the rules? Is your sense of fairness tightly associated with your personal identity? You need to find out.

What are you really angry at? If it's not the object of your passion, could it be an unsettled argument within?

Acknowledging the emotion that arises and noticing the temptation of the distraction of blame is a basic tool of self-discovery. This is called being honest with ourselves. When we are honest about our true emotions, we can begin to search for the resentments that compel them.

Anger, like all emotions, is available to us for the choosing. Yes, there is a choice. It happens very fast. Our choice is to dwell in anger or not. Like other painful emotions, our false sense of personality gets triggered because our Third Part has led us to a situation to give us an opportunity to uncover buried truths. There, this opportunity exists to discover painful realizations instead of attaching to the seeming relief of blame.

This is not a problem to solve. It is a path to discover. When we have discovered one trigger and its ensuing distraction habit, another will come along. This isn't a process of not feeling pain or not having pain; it is the process of recognizing where the pain comes from.

What eventually ensues is a calming of the mind as it realizes the futility of endlessly fighting to ward off the pain hidden in our repressed emotions.

Diversions-distractions from truth turn into compulsions to hide from truth.

Often, our denial of pain and our method for avoiding it is from childhood. Years of avoidance can hide a troubling situation far below the conscious mind's daily observance.

One of the most common avoidance pitfalls is having an exciting cover-up. The mind can devise some compelling alternatives to exploring pain. These distractions may serve so often to replace our divinity with anxiety that we think it's normal. It is not. You are a Divine being.

Nothing very deep will be eliminated overnight. It takes diligent and persistent effort to identify the pain we are avoiding. A spiritual life is a step-by-step process.

Like turning the pages of a book or following a trail,
there will always be something new to discover.

Recognize our Emotional Pain

This is not a pain in the body. It is a pain in the Soul. Doubts, fears, and the like are part of our existence. Anguish, anger, anxiety ... the list goes on.

We often find ourselves wallowing in these places. It seems impossible to will them away or prohibit their return. Sometimes, we feel as though we have escaped from them. We cover them up, deny their existence, and try to move on. How would it be to assess these disturbances not as problems but as confusions? What if we are not wrong, just unprepared?

We can sift through this confusion only after we admit to its existence.

Acknowledge all your pain.

Feel the shock of the pain.

Accept that others are in pain.

If you're confused, whether you realize it or not, the peace you crave will arrive when the true source of the pain is found.

Repeat problems show the way.

What we see as problems are just states of confusion seen through the lens of pain. We all have areas of confusion that have a common thread: a recurrence of some outward phenomena has repeatedly caused confusion, such as unhealthy habits like rage or hate.

A Soul problem means that a spiritual truth has been denied or avoided. Part of this spiritual truth exists inside us. Confusion occurs when another part of our being is not in alignment. This constant absence of truth causes us the pain of disunity, separation within ourselves. We continue to experience this disunity or pain as long as we avoid accepting that spiritual truth.

We should not look at what's wrong with us but rather the deep-seated need or fear we haven't yet acknowledged.

Whatever brought about these false ideas, acknowledging their power in our lives is the first and maybe the only step we need to take to relieve ourselves of their torment.

Blame is the only sin.

Why? Because blame robs us of the opportunity to see ourselves as the powerful creator beings we really are.

We cannot simultaneously be powerful and blame others. The first step to realizing our power is taking full responsibility for all our actions, thoughts, and emotions.

When we blame others, we are telling ourselves that we are helpless and that the other person's actions are controlling our thoughts and behavior.

This is not the truth. Their actions may have triggered a response in us. But it is *our* response.

Affirmation

"I do not blame anyone for how I feel. I am deeply aware of my negative emotions. I resolve to be open to the source of these emotions. I believe that at the source of these emotions lie memories I have not accepted because I fear their pain. When I am ready and willing, acceptance will find me."

5

REDUCING THE RELIANCE ON PRETENSE

You are not your personality.

The typical adaptation we all make to living in the physical and mental worlds is to create an outward personality that will presumably provide the approval and acceptance we seek.

When conflicts and uncertainties arise in our thoughts, a process begins where we feel ashamed of our supposed weaknesses. To counteract this feeling, the True Self is drawn back, and a false self is shown to the world. I call this false self a pretense.

This false self of personality is not inherently good or evil. Through the pretense of personality, we may engage in acts of kindness and generosity, demonstrating to the world that we are lovable. At other times, we may act aggressively or submissively. We present this pretend self to others as if it is who we are.

The false self dwells in the past and future, relying on incorrect conclusions about the past to promote a desirable future. This prevents us from living in the present, where the Third Part dwells.

The irony is that as much as we may want to believe our false self is making us happy in this charade, the pretense personality can never be happy. Deep inside, the truth of its false fabrication will hinder any joy, disregard any accomplishment, and even deny receiving love. We feel unloved because the True Self is hidden, unavailable to give love or receive love from others.

Some people live their entire lives in misery, complaining about the world's cruelties and never realizing that this pretense personality is *pretend*—a lie, the false self. After suffering from the neglect of not showing their True Self, some begin to see the ineffectiveness of this pretense.

Most of us will not be able to dissolve this pretentious act completely, but even recognizing its existence is a valuable step toward revealing our true nature.

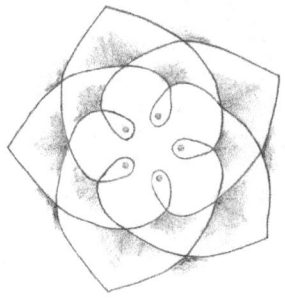

There are some problems that we can't seem to solve. But what if we can look deeper?

What if we give ourselves a superficial problem and notice why we can't solve it?

Answering this question helps us find out if there are hidden motivations behind the way we live our lives. This is not an exercise about success or failure in solving a problem. It's an exercise to reveal the inner workings of your mind by bringing what has been hidden from your awareness to a focal point where you can examine it.

Here is an experiment I want you to try. Tell yourself that you are going to abstain from a habit that is putting your health at risk—smoking, drinking alcohol, eating too much sugar, or what have you. Or perhaps you prefer to do this experiment from the perspective of trying something new, like doing yoga, volunteering, or being nicer to someone. Either way, tell yourself that you will make this change in your life for three days. Use your willpower to convince yourself of your sincere commitment to this decision. Once you have made a firm commitment to make a change, notice what comes up when you start thinking about this adjustment to your life routine.

Almost immediately, the decision to interfere with your habits, either letting one go or trying to add something new, shifts some part of your mind into a cautionary mode that begins plotting how to get back to the comfort zone of your old pattern and routine. Notice the insidious nature of this plotting. Listen for the mind's increasingly desperate bribes, accusations, and pleadings. You may even see a connection to some childhood pain anchoring your resistance to change.

Remember, this is not about how effective your willpower is; it's about how receptive you can be to the emotional turmoil this threat to normalcy creates. You must accept the existence of these rational parts of who you are, without defensiveness or guilt, to be able to leave them behind for good.

This exercise also works well with other problem areas in your life. For example, if you have money problems, you might try making a firm decision to tithe by donating some percentage or set amount of your income to charity every time you receive money. Watch how your mind responds to this idea. Be prepared for unending mental explanations about how, just this one time, doing good for yourself by holding on to the money is better than doing good for others. If that comes up, there's a chance that fear is controlling your inner dialog.

Here's how this exercise worked for me. I decided I would give up eating sugar. I won't go into the long list of foods containing sugar that I frequently ate. Save it to say that I had to try some new foods just so I wasn't hungry.

After the first day of avoiding sugar, I convinced myself that my first successes in abstention should be rewarded by, you guessed it, a sugary snack. I also found that after a heated internal argument about how much sugar I was avoiding, I tried to convince myself of how mindful I was becoming and soon would not need to carry out this stupid experiment.

I told myself that this exercise was a waste of time, nothing good would come of it, and as soon as I ate whatever I wanted, all my problems would be gone. This agonizing debate became the window through which I could watch my mind rebel against a new idea. It also helped me recognize this same resistant inner voice at other times when an inspiration required me to change a habit or try something different.

In your response to the suggestion of trying this experiment, perhaps you're thinking something like this.

Sure, this is a great idea. But I don't have to really do it because I already know what's going to happen.

This is the kind of rationalization that keeps you stuck in the same place on constant repeat, reliving the same patterns over and over again because the mind refuses to let you out of its grip. What you think might happen if you do this experiment and what's really going to happen are two entirely different things. One is the supposed satisfaction of being so clever; the other is an enlightening event that might lead you to look at your life from a different perspective.

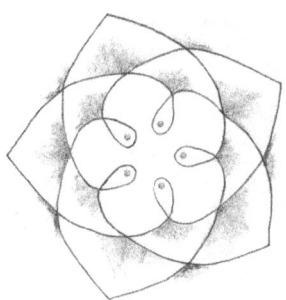

The voice of habit can be recognized.

Here's a little story about how, with practice, we learn to recognize the hidden voice of habit.

When robocalling first happened on my home phone, I'd answer the phone thinking it was someone I knew. This was my habit.

Time after time, though, I had to hang up on some salesperson or a recorded marketing call. This is recognizing that the habit has drawbacks.

It wasn't long before I recognized a pattern in the timing of the calls or some other indicator that made me hesitate to answer. I started questioning whether I should pick up the phone when it rang. I couldn't make the calls stop, but at least I could work on my response to them. This is making a choice instead of unquestioningly following a habit. I know you have all had the same or similar experiences of changing your habits.

Once you can tell the difference between the voice of the habit and the guidance from the Third Part, many of your beliefs about life are brought to light—exposed and open to review.

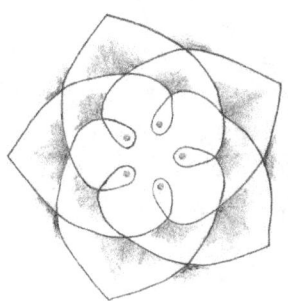

Have we been living in a dream where
we think we have all the answers,
or is there space for inspiration to be heard?

There is no end to the opportunities to see through the habit of our illusions. Try putting this book down now and notice if one of your compulsions immediately comes to mind—eating food, checking your phone, distracting house chores. Every revelation of the hidden motivation behind these compulsions brings you one step closer to having your True Self operating in its place.

The mobile interconnected device we all carry around is the latest gift from Oneness to get us to see how much pain it might cost to just put the thing away for a while. Yes, there is something we are longing for, but we won't find it on the internet.

Do you hate politics? No, you don't. Something on the political landscape has triggered a deep-seated resentment. Something assumed to be very painful has re-occurred inside, not outside. Blasting away at perceived disunity in the outer world is a symptom of the Soul's desire for inner harmony.

Boss, kids, spouse, bothering you? Try again. It really is something you are not letting go of. These angels are working with you to find a more peaceful place for all. Won't you help?

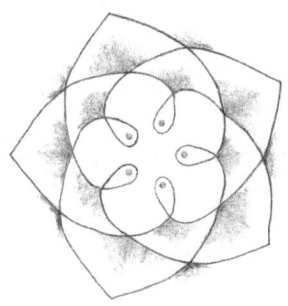

Relax. Life is not a test.

Nor is it a game we can win or lose. The beauty of living life at the Soul level is that we begin to recognize and accept the compulsive, protective self with grace. Living in a more peaceful state allows us to perceive our True Self.

The mind is not easily silenced, nor should it be. It is an ally for navigating the world that is not easily subdued through willpower or hopeful practices. But as we become more in alignment with the Third Part, the mind releases the need for overstimulated protection, and its usefulness in cooperating with the other parts of our being becomes natural.

Once we see through the illusion of our mind's compulsions, it changes who we are. We become open to accepting solutions different from the ones we thought were working for us.

Don't expect overnight success in overcoming habits of the mind—protective or otherwise. You may have had these hidden habitual motivations for many lifetimes. But over time, these compulsions can fade away. You may not even notice their absence until one day you wake up feeling strength in a part of you where before was weakness or ignorance.

The good news is that the Third Part knows the path to our True Self and is always present to show us the way. When we listen, we grow. Eventually, compulsions relinquish their hold on us. This shift may have a seemingly magical quality, but it is just us becoming more reliant on the power of the Third Part as a very real and noticeable presence in our lives.

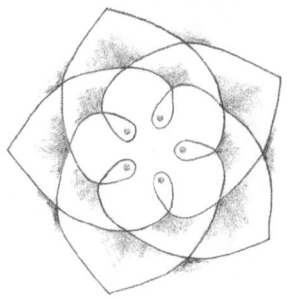

Being present means being less in the past and less in the future.

Enticing distractions of the past are anger, shame, regret, and guilt.

Enticing distractions of the future are fear, desire, and expectations.

These are *time-based* distractions. They rely on a fictitious illusion of believing that we can live in two places at once. We are alive only in the present moment.

Noticing if the mind is repeatedly dwelling on certain memories or future concerns can lead to inspection of their origin in some mistaken belief.

Noticing the voice that brings these distracting illusions to mind provides an opportunity to learn how to distinguish the habitual-mind voice from the voice of inspiration.

Accepting the futility of our perceived expectations based on dwelling in the past and future allows us to be present, to notice and align with what may be surprising circumstances that hardly seem possible.

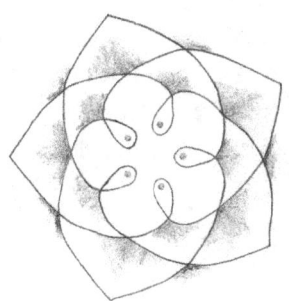

Moment by Moment, Many Times a Second

Experiments have shown that the brain's response time to a visual cue is a mere 1/10 of a second and could be faster at different times and in different people.

Here's an experiment you can do at home.

Breathe.

As you breathe, notice the difference in how your body feels on the inhale and exhale. Notice which muscles are engaged at each inflow and outflow of breath. Try to notice that tiny moment when the muscles engaged in the inhale give way to the muscles engaged in the exhale. Can you feel one muscle group relax as the other group takes over? Can you connect your awareness with that small moment in between the shift?

This is just one of the many tiny moments that make up our existence. Some are body maintenance, such as heartbeat, staying balanced, and the iris adjusting to light. Some are triggers. Some are questions. Some are Divine interventions. Merely acknowledging the existence of the phenomenon prepares us to take a closer examination of each moment.

Recognizing the momentary shift between your in and out breaths demonstrates that you have the ability to recognize each moment of your existence in other aspects of your life. It just takes practice to sharply focus your attention and notice the tiny details that escape us when we are distracted.

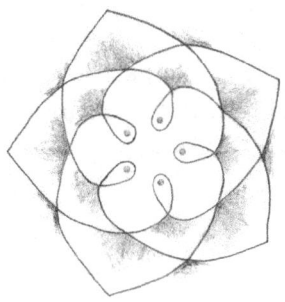

Living in the moment is difficult because there are so many of them.

We all have difficulty staying in the present moment.

The mind's incessant wandering especially makes this seem like no easy task.

Some say just let thoughts evaporate like clouds. Sounds easy until they keep coming back like a winter storm.

My preference is to notice whether I'm dwelling on past events or future plans. I ask myself if I am afraid or excited. Taking notice of the moment between having a thought that inspires action and taking that action allows me to observe my mind. I have observed a great hesitancy of my mind to release its infatuation with the past and future, revealing clues about my true beliefs and motivations.

I find that this inquiry takes away the momentum of the distractions, calming my mind until I can reorient myself to the present moment.

Yes, distracting thoughts return, but they become less frequent and less consuming. Some think that the ability to be in the present moment is a tiring exercise. But I feel a calmness when residing in the present.

This practice can be difficult to do, and continuing it when there isn't much improvement is a challenge. But, an ongoing curiosity and an appreciation for the short bursts of peace that occur in these moments of self-reflection increases the ability to shift into the present moment and prolong the stay.

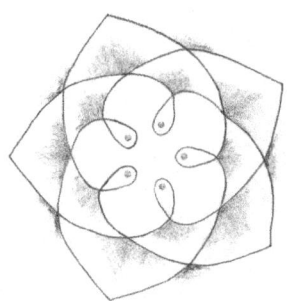

Willpower

Will vs. Intent is a matter of time preconception.

Willpower is the illusion of time—a confusion between the present moment and the future. Relying on the ability to construct the future through force of will renders us almost useless in the present moment. It is not possible to construct a future outcome that does not yet exist in the present moment.

At most, we may have an intention. The power of intention, however, is that, unlike willpower, it is not tied to a specific outcome. Instead, it merely serves as a guide, opening us to the possibilities that may unfold through our Universal interconnectedness.

Stop using your willpower.
Start using your willpower.

For six years, I taught sailing to kids in their early teens at a summer camp run by a local parks and recreation department. One of the skills I taught my students was how to tack. In short, tacking is turning the boat. It is somewhat like making a right or left-hand turn with your car at an intersection. Like the steering wheel in the car, the boat rudder is used to begin and complete the turn. But making the turn in water is much harder because no painted stripes or curbs provide a directional guide for navigating the turn to the new course.

On the first day of class, when the kids were practicing tacking, I was always telling them one of two things.

"Keep turning! Keep turning!" when they were not yet on course.

Or "Stop turning! Stop turning!" when they had turned past course.

Eventually, through the trial and error of making corrections, my students learned how to find the new course. Our willpower is like the rudder; it can be underused or overused. Consistently noticing the results of our actions and knowing when to use our willpower to make corrections keeps us on course.

What you can't change with your willpower is your emotions, beliefs, or habits.

What you can change with your willpower is your awareness, resolve, and intentions.

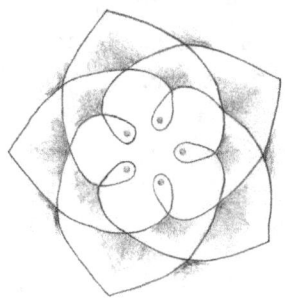

Quit trying to be holy.
Give up pretense and be yourself.

Please try not to invent another personality while using these practices. Your True Self is the goal; there's no reason to create more obstacles by substituting one pretense for another. This process is not asking you to act like a saint or look like a monk. When exploring your inner self, there is no requirement for a serious or solemn approach.

When I start falling into traps of believing I need to do something or be someone better, I think of Aikido. Don't resist. But be aware and let the perceived benefits of false betterment flow past me as I step aside. This allows me to stay focused and aware of my eternal goals and the inevitability of more traps.

We all question whether to listen or act on certain thoughts. As we continue to engage in practices to lower the allure of pretense, we gain the certainty and sustainability of our True Selves as our guide. Our options become clearer, and decisions are easier to make.

We don't need ceremonies, scriptures, and icons to hear the messages that come from Oneness. With our True Self as our guide, we will know what is true. What we need to support our highest and best good is waiting for us to allow it to appear in our lives.

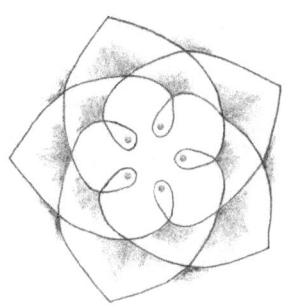

6

IF IT'S NOT A SURPRISE, IT'S NOT GOD TALKING

Every problem is a Soul problem.

The basic situation on Earth is that our species continues to rely on sensory data to exist in an ethereal realm. Not only is this a source of confusion about what is, but also of frustration about what can be done.

A personal story that illustrates this point relates back to when I was a truck driver with my own truck. On this occasion, I had been sent to the Oakland docks to pick up a shipping container. I was waiting in a line of trucks and turned my truck engine off. When the line started moving forward, the engine would not start after repeated attempts. Finding no mechanical solution to the problem, I returned to my truck cab and sat in silence to reflect on my current situation. I needed the money this job provided, but the work stagnated my efforts to improve my life and career. I was at a crossroads, knowing in my heart that I should be doing something else, yet feeling a powerful drive to be competent and even loyal to what I was doing. It was truly a deeply emotional moment questioning my existence.

In that moment, I stopped trying to think my way through the problem and relaxed into a meditative state. I was instantly filled with a sense of conviction for a greater purpose in life and felt the resilience of my inner self to succeed in finding a way forward to fulfill that purpose. I felt very light and courageous. Then, I had a dreamlike vision of turning my truck around and leaving the container business. Arising from that reflective moment, I pressed the starter button, and the engine responded immediately. I turned the truck around and never went back.

I offer this personal anecdote to illustrate that we may not be aware of having powerful, intuitive energy within ourselves. Though we have some inkling of our intuitive abilities, we find it difficult to accept and acknowledge them on a day-to-day basis. Some are afraid of this power and what it might unleash within them. Some are afraid that it will take them out of their comfort zone. For some, believing in another reality beyond what the physical senses and logical mind can perceive and understand is unimaginable. Still, others may feel that results from using intuition are unlikely and not worth the effort.

Perhaps you have a problem with money, addictions, relationships, or other difficult challenges. I can assure you that if you've been trying very hard for a long time and have seen little results, there is an underlying confusion about the reality in which a solution may be found. I call this a Soul problem. Rather than looking to external solutions, I believe the answer to these problems resides within us. These external problems are not in our true nature. They are symptoms.

Perhaps by following some of the practices in this book, you will begin to know and accept the Third Part of your Divine being. As you continue to support your true nature, external problems naturally resolve in alignment with your inner truth.

The Third Part knows the way.

It is not true that you need to look for or to find God. What God is for you is already within you.

We have been on this path for a while. Do not confuse your present dissatisfactions with your past performance. Each of us has overcome many obstacles through the centuries and lives we have witnessed. Our growth is real, and our achievements are too numerous to list.

I am on a hunt for the distractions that keep me from my goal of unity consciousness. These distractions are caused by confusion, not evil. Once I admit to the distraction, I trust that the Third Part can more easily guide my purposes without the need for persuasion.

Enlightenment is not something we need to look for in hopes of finding it; it is something the Third Part knows we cannot avoid.

Our past can be with us in the present moment.

Some wonder if it is necessary to re-live the past in order to solve present dilemmas. The truth is that the past never leaves. All our erroneous beliefs brought about by past circumstances are available in the present. Some call this *karma*.

Each present moment arrives with the ability to be in any place and time. The confusion of the past, if not unwoven by practical insight, may keep influencing our daily decisions. The choice to take responsibility for every thought and every emotion exists in the present moment. Pick any thought as it races by. Is it a clear and unprejudiced thought based on the present moment, or is it a remnant of some past experience, recalling need, anger, or jealousy?

Acknowledging responsibility for each emotion as it arises in the present moment avoids creating more confusion.

Be calm. There is no need to examine every disturbance. Our problems are not going anywhere that we can't find them. At your leisure, in meditation, or walking in nature, any honest attempt to reconcile the present moment from the emotions of your past is a worthy pursuit.

Faster Consciousness

The Universe vibrates on multiple frequencies. The Third Part resonates with the eternal rhythms. By comparison, our mind vibrates at a slower frequency, and our body vibrates even more slowly.

I use faster rather than higher to describe the nature of vibrational consciousness because it is a more approachable adjective. By this, I mean faster is a word one can approach in a practical way; its normal use implies incremental change. In comparison, higher presupposes a sense of duality—higher or lower.

Consider the pace of our mind—how fast the mind can move from one thought to the next. Consider also the slower pace of the mind when dwelling on an unfortunate circumstance or superficial pleasure. Often, habit keeps us from moving from one thought to another. Recognizing the difference between dwelling and eager curiosity opens the mind's awareness to the moment.

We have a choice over the pace of our mind, including accepting the faster pace of our Third Part. The Third Part does not slow down to give previews, make promises, or persuade.

We all have had these experiences of a quickening realization. They are part of our eternal being.

Immediate Acceptance

The Universal rhythms of Oneness arrive in our consciousness with the price of immediate acceptance.

One has just a moment to align intention with inspiration.

The words that have been passed down are *the moment of truth.* Is this a moment when you take a leap of faith, or is it a moment when you hesitate?

The mind has the inertia of protectiveness, constantly portraying our inspirations as suspicious. Just a few moments trapped in this habitual doubting can cause inspiration from Oneness to be lost.

Realizing that inspiration can be a momentary passing may be motivation for increasing our awareness and honesty of what is on our minds.

For me, this motivation helps with practicing patience. Patience is letting go of expectations and calms the mind, allowing immediate acceptance to align with inspiration.

Inspiration, by definition, is a surprise.

What is a surprise? In my view, it's an event that we hadn't thought of or even imagined would happen. I also incorporate the idea of creativity in art, spontaneity in conversation, and inspiration in thought in the definition of surprise. Humor is a surprise. Good comedy is storytelling with surprise endings.

Of course, *God talking* is merely an analogy. Inspiration arrives as unexpected newness and must come from previously unexplored patterns of thought. Our willingness to accept the unexplored and sometimes unreasonable thoughts and emotions allows us to participate in opening ourselves to unimagined possibilities.

The inspiration-surprise is often foreign to our normal way of thinking. We may question an idea as a mystery because we can't resolve the outcome. Here is the frontier of living a life where unresolved ideas may lead to the transformation of a previously held mistaken belief.

We have all heard the saying, "God works in mysterious ways." Perhaps it's not mysterious but revealing truths we have not yet come to accept. The power of accepting inspiration is a breakthrough; it dissolves my determination to be entitled to my expectation of a desired outcome.

When we avoid the unknown, we avoid inspiration.

Our preference for the familiar is genetically embedded in the preservation of our physical bodies. When this preference becomes our operational standard in the Soul realm, we become cut off from inspiration.

Our opinions are often rigid. When our view of the known is faced with a surprising event, it's often met with pain or fear. Our mind goes into *intruder alert* mode as it tests the validity of the new idea against pre-established standards of the known.

You've heard of tortured artists. Just what tortures them? Could it be their constant struggle to reject the restraints of preconceived programming that frees them, opening them to receive inspiration?

I experienced a lot of fears as inspiration challenged my beliefs; my mind would hesitate. Each mental *No* was attached to fear. It took courage to accept the unknown.

I've come to rely on an expectation of surprise. The ineffectiveness of my repeating the same decisions led me to explore other methods of progress. An original thought must break rigid, habitual prejudices.

The joy of creativity is the joy of letting go.

Alignment of your whole being

We have the capacity to be consciously creative beings, to receive inspiration, recognize it, act on it, and contribute to the Earth's well-being. What stands in our way?

Our body has not been subject to the presumptuous concerns of our mind. The will to live, avoid pain, and grow is inherent, unassailable, and natural. The messages we receive from our bodies are innate ancient wisdom. Simply put, our body lives in truth.

The Third Part of our being enjoys a constant connection to universal wisdom. It is unhampered by desire or worry. It, too, holds truth.

How can we align the mind with these truths?

Here's an example of non-alignment. I have just entered a room filled with people I don't know. My body knows I am nervous; it sends these signals to my mind. The Third Part recognizes the unfamiliar situation is a learning experience. But what is my mind doing? Either it's pretending that everything is perfect or reacting in fear that disaster awaits—neither aligns with the truths that my body and the Third Part are telling me.

Another example. I am walking along a street. I see a beggar. My body remembers what it is like to be hungry and cold. The Third Part opens to the opportunity of receiving compassion. Is the mind lost in insufficiency, lack, and embarrassment, unable to move into compassion? This is not alignment.

Just one more. I see someone, and they hold my attention for a moment. My body senses warmth, closeness, and familiarity. The Third Part recognizes the insubstantiality of separateness. Can the mind overcome the belief of being rejected or misunderstood? What would happen if the three parts came into alignment?

It may be difficult to align the mind with the messages from our body and the Third Part. Being out of alignment prevents our acceptance of the reality of the moment. The truth we seek is within us, calling to us, showing us a place where the confused mind can come into alignment with the truth.

The Oneness that we long for is the alignment of our whole being. When the three parts of our being are in agreement, unimagined inspiration can arrive. Some call this magic. It is not magic. It is the profound simplicity of the true nature of being whole.

It is not for me to say how your mind will come into alignment. We each have our own misunderstandings, prejudices, and buried emotions. How these are brought into the light will be different for everyone. Consciously accepting our natural resistance to change is essential.

7

PRAYERS AND INTENTIONS

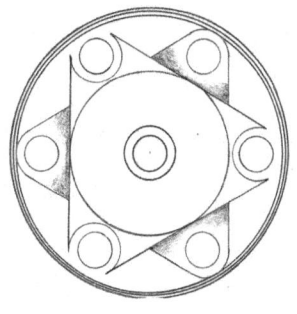

Managing Intentions

In every moment, we hold an intention. We may not always be aware of what our intentions are or the motivation behind them.

An intention may originate from the mind or from the Third Part. The difference between the intentions of the mind and the Third Part is that the intentions of the Third Part do not rely on an outcome.

Having an intention is different than having a plan. Intentions of the Third Part are not about what we intend to do or get but who we intend to be. An intention places the importance of purpose above results. Plans usually have goals or expectations.

If you have held the same plan for a long time, picturing the same perfect outcome for your life, you are interfering with the expression of your true nature.

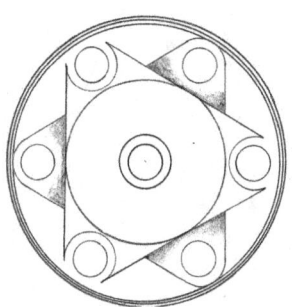

How can I cooperate with my Soul's purpose?

Our Soul's purpose is not what we think it is, nor will it lead us to a pre-determined destination. On this path, the only destination is change—we change. What we change into is not a matter of choice. Try not to imagine or decide what the Third Part is or what it means to reach enlightenment.

What are you hoping for, wishing for? How long has this been going on? Have you been sucked into the promises of prosperity? Have fantasies of success and riches seeped into your wise and beautiful heart? To move forward, you must let go of these outcomes.

Having a focus on earthly desires obscures the Soul's purpose. The moment I let the Third Part guide me and surrender to surprise, I transition from being bound to my desires to being free to serve my Soul's purpose.

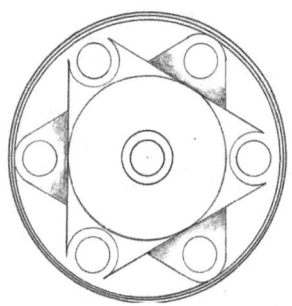

Intentions need accuracy to change behavior.

Much confusion in life can be eliminated by realizing the difference between a trigger, an emotion, and an intention.

Feeling insulted is a trigger. Getting angry is an emotion. Wanting revenge is an intention.

Feeling complimented is a trigger. Being satisfied is an emotion. Wanting to be kind to others is an intention.

Our actions and behaviors are a result of our intentions. Intentions are a result of our emotions. Careful consideration of our emotional state and examination of the preceding triggers brings accurate awareness of intentions.

This is not about how hard we try. It's about how honest we are.

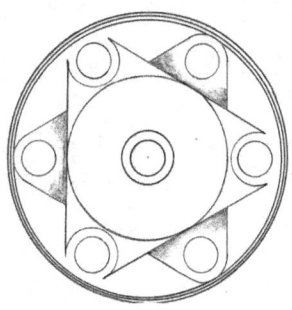

Faith, Strength, and Perseverance

Faith, strength, and perseverance are already ours. They are tools that we possess.

When I do yoga, I practice awareness of the position of my bones and the stress on my muscles. After years of practicing postures, I was delighted to find that I had become aware of the smallest details. One of those minute details was noticing the strength of the muscles I was holding tight and the ones that were relaxed. Focusing on this balance gave me the perseverance to hold the yoga position.

When I started yoga, I thought I would have to use all my strength to remain in a position. But as I became more skilled, I was surprised to find that relaxed focus and patience have as much to do with having the perseverance to hold a pose as strength does.

The more I relied on focus and patience, the more I felt a renewed strength.

Patience takes courage and willpower not to act until you are sure that the volition is willfully given without premeditation of fear or expectations of delight.

Laziness, most assume, is a mental problem. However, it is a manifestation of the lack of faith. At the core is a lack of faith in oneself. Willpower cannot stop laziness because it's not a problem of will. It is a problem of faith.

No worries. Faith is in you. You will learn to recognize it. Believe in it. And act on it.

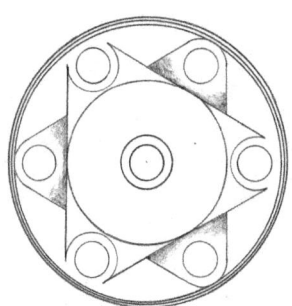

Prayer has gotten a bad reputation.

I understand the reluctance that some feel about petitioning an undetermined entity.

When we're praying for what we think we need, we aren't open to what the Third Part is ready to provide.

It doesn't make a difference to my notion of God whether I call out, "Dear, Lord" or "Hey baby, I need you now." What matters is what I am asking in calling out to God. Am I asking for a vacation, a new car, or the strength and courage to face the next moment with honesty and conviction?

Prayer can be asking the Universe to change so it fits our expectations, or it can be asking to be in connection with the Universe as it is.

I don't ask for what I need. I figure that the Third Part knows what I need. I would rather receive and take part in the gifts that it provides.

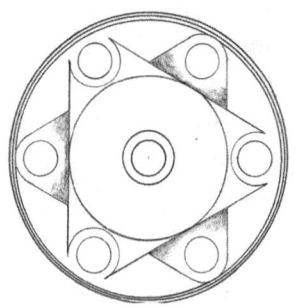

Prayers can be an insight into our distractions as well as a source of calmness.

Prayers, chants, affirmations, mantras, and hymns can allow inner dialogue to surface for inspection and provide relief for a troubled mind.

When making these recitations, we are repeating a memorized phrase over and over again. Within moments after starting the recitations, many of us find that some part of our mind has begun to wander, thinking about other things. The distractions are many—hunger, pain, emotions, internal musings, ruminations, worry, and more.

In some practices, one is told that these distracting thoughts are impediments to peace within. The hope is that practicing the prayer will somehow overcome the distractions, and they will fall away. But these supposed impediments to peace also offer great insights into truths about ourselves, our minds, habits, and fears if we are willing to look within for their source.

It is one thing to acknowledge fear. It is quite another to search for the source of the fear. Just having the intention to one day understand our motivations opens the door to the path of self-discovery. If acted on, that intention brings us closer to our True Selves. The way out from the burden of mental concerns has never been through forcibly trying to overcome them. But rather by leaning into them, examining them to find the truth within.

Still, at times, the internal discourse can be overwhelming. The mind's passion for control in response to being examined is very devious, leading us to believe that only certain topics are worthy of attention, such as others' wrongdoings, what others think of us, our appearance, and how much money we have, don't have, or want.

This is when staying focused on a unifying thought to soothe the mind's turmoil can be useful. When I need this kind of focus, I sing love songs. You may prefer Sanskrit mantras, new-age affirmations, hymns, sacred readings, native chants, or myriad other ways we can focus the mind.

There will be times in the angst of daily life when you try some practice for calming the mind, and your mind says *No,* again and again, refusing to submit to any interference with its superiority in choosing the object of focus. Then, one time, without even a moment's hesitation, your perseverance and courage will hold sway over your mind's insistence on superiority. You will feel that mantra, that song, that prayer arrive quietly, without expectation, bringing calm and inner peace. Once you experience the awareness of this inner strength to overcome the mind's control, you will never be the same.

The mind's passion will overcome your intentions many more times. But if you persevere, your inner strength will grow.

The peace we seek is not that far away; it's just behind the fearful mind.

Allow the Third Part to bring you back to this place of strength.

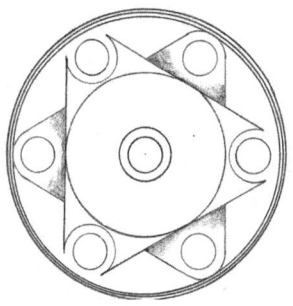

You are Oneness. You are praying to yourself.

There is a place of resonance within us: the Third Part's connection to Oneness. In this connection, separation dissolves, and we are one with all there is. Our prayers are a process of strengthening this connection.

What phrase, prayer, or song is best to find your inner strength? Ask. Have an intention of opening to find your personal message. This will allow it to appear to your awareness. You will know it when you find it.

The perfect prayer, affirmation, or song for the moment is always available to you. It may be in a book or something you read on the internet. It might come from a friend or something you hear on the radio.

With joyfulness, see these gifts as treasures to add to your personal songbook of prayers.

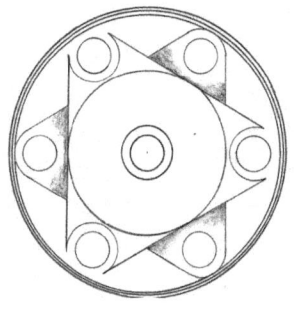

8

PATIENCE
AND CREATIVITY

Perseverance, Motivation, and the Olive Grove

I once had a piece of property and decided to grow olive trees to produce olive oil. Without a lot of capital, I resorted to buying very small starter plants in one-gallon planters at eight bucks apiece. I bought eighty of them. The plants were as thin as pencils, barely two feet tall, with a few tiny branches and a handful of leaves. It's difficult to describe how impossible it seemed that these twig-like plants would grow into trees and produce olives.

Still, when I got the plants home, I dug holes for them, planted them in healthy soil, and ran irrigation lines.

By the first year, the plants had grown into small bushes. I pruned them for structure, pulled weeds, and watered them when appropriate. I tended these plants for four years without ever seeing one olive. Finally, by the fifth year, each plant produced a few olives. I was overjoyed. However, my mentor told me that I had to pull them all off immediately to allow the tree to use its energy for root and branch development. Sad to strip the plants of their fruit, I followed the instruction.

Much to my delight, the following year brought many blossoms that turned into olive buds. But this time, I did not have to strip off the budding olives. Eventually, they matured until they were ready for harvest.

After harvesting the olives, I took them to a processor to be ground and filtered to produce the oil. I call myself a writer, but there is no way I can describe the feelings and emotions I experienced when I saw my name on the bottles of olive oil. I had never felt this way. Satisfaction, rewarded, competent, all the words were inadequate.

But the true elation happened much later, out in the orchard, as I continued with the care and maintenance of the olive trees. Until then, my work in the orchard was satisfying, based on hope—on the future. Now, the vision of those bottles supported me in a way that lifted the work of pruning and weeding to a different level. I could feel it in my heart, in my feet, and in my hands. It was less tiring. I looked up to see the sky. I listened to the birds. I could taste the oil.

I was transformed. Motivation came from a different place. No longer was it from thinking what might be possible. I wasn't unsure if my efforts would produce success. The motivation came effortlessly from the realization of results.

Can you persevere for two years?

In my experience, there is a period of time before one notices the real effect of bringing the Third Part into balance with the rest of our being. One must be prepared for this interim of questioning and validation. Although each person's timing is different, two years is a realistic expectation.

Does two years sound like a long time? Too long for you to even begin a transformation of your life? How many years is your car loan? Your education? Your relationships? The question is, how can you expect remarkable results overnight? Perhaps you have spent years trying different paths and have given up on them because the results you expected did not arrive when you thought they should.

Let's get back once more to the motivation to incorporate the Third Part in your daily life. It takes time for noticeable results to be your motivation. Before that, much must be taken on faith. Or logic. Or, let's face it, desperation.

It's not so much that progress is not being made. It's that it takes time to adjust to noticing the improvement. If you plant an olive tree, you can't see its day-to-day growth. But after a while, you'll notice how much it's grown.

You may not be able to notice infinitesimal changes in your consciousness. But it's happening. The Third Part is always acting on your behalf. Do not be distracted by searching for proof that change is happening. Results come in abrupt and surprising ways, not because we are looking for them.

Notice the calm. At first, this may only be noticed as cracks in the confusion, short-lived and rare. Your intention to discover your truth will be found in the cracks. The cracks will eventually grow into chasms of longer moments, and there will be more of them.

Even in the depths of sorrow, which is inevitable, you will begin to rely on the reoccurrence of calm.

Joy is not the absence of hardship;
joy is the acceptance of hardship.

Realizing a state of hardship, one is tempted to resort to compunctions of remedy. Temporary distractions give us an illusion of joy. Sooner or later, the present moment catches up with the illusion, and the hardship remains.

The expectation of ease fuels disappointment in the face of hardship. Life does not get easier; all our problems do not go away. But through them, we learn to understand the true nature of courage. We gain strength in our ability to accept our inner turmoil. There is joy in knowing our strength.

Having fewer desires, compulsions, and avoidances results in joy.

Joy is a great motivator. It makes space for creativity, replacing the complacency of habit in facing hardship.

Be prepared for sadness.
Sadness is not the opposite of joy.

Sadness is my word for an emotion that is without remorse, guilt, or shame. When I finally see and understand the distractions of a habit or reaction I have held onto, I feel sadness in knowing how much I have mistakenly relied on it to steer my life's course. It is a temporary sadness. Joy is eternal.

My sadness lies in the realization that the distractions were my way of escaping from pain I couldn't bear to feel. When I uncovered the pain, experiencing sadness was a necessary part of accepting that pain. The pain passes. Joy is eternal.

Acceptance of our distractions and pain enables us to align our body, mind, and the Third Part. The body feels the sadness. The Soul realizes the sadness. The mind accepts the temporary situation as a lesson on our path.

The small flame of joy becomes powerful when viewed as eternal.

When I found my joy, it wasn't very big, which, of course, made it very difficult to find. There were times when I even forgot that I had any.

Then I realized joy is eternal. It has always been there. It always will be.

There are times when joy looms large in my world; still, there are other times when it appears quite small. But now I don't forget that I have it.

The more I practice finding joy, the sooner I remember it's always there.

Eternal Patience

Can you feel that eternal part of yourself, if only for a moment? Can you see your confusion as a temporary state of learning?

After we have discovered some of the confused, underlying motivations that have been running our lives, we are able to discern the truth and clarity of the Third Part, which has always been in our consciousness.

The Third Part's resiliency and intentions have been with us throughout our existence. Only when we are lost in our confusion does it seem like the mind is all we are.

Round and round, the wheel of life turns from having confidence in the Third Part to succumbing to our confusion, illusions, and errors and back to confidence again.

When this cycle of growth becomes automatic, and we can see both the confidence and the confusion at work, our patience will grow, allowing us to rely on constant and eternal access to truth in each moment.

Eternal Creativity

The Third Part offers a way out of our addictions and our illusions. At first, it may not occur to us that there could be another solution beyond our hardened determination. Turning to patience is more than being calm. It is a reliance on the Third Part's innate longing to provide an answer.

Creativity is the ability to notice and allow the Third Part's surprising plan to manifest. Patience is the ability to wait for it.

Patience—not force. Creativity—not habit. When force is the choice being considered, it's time for patience. When habit is the choice, it's time for creativity.

Substituting creativity for habit initially feels like loss.

Substituting patience for force initially feels like weakness.

You'll get over it.

Even when life is difficult,
that doesn't mean you're wrong.

The true path of life goes through difficult times. This doesn't mean this is the wrong path. Sometimes, the most difficult emotions come at a time when a breakthrough is near. These difficulties appear when awareness has arrived at the truth of a matter—a truth that may have been avoided until this moment.

Maybe these difficult times can be greeted with a different attitude. Take a breath; stand tall. Is there an opening for a surprise? Our lives cannot be made whole by the mind's need for control, brought on by fear of change, which sees growth as disaster.

Fall down, weep, then get up. This is not a mistake. This is an improvement.

The spiritual part will succeed without aggression, pride, or remorse.

We cannot avoid enlightenment.

After we calm the addictions to distraction and still the need for immediate results, we can use will to pry open our concerns. This must be done in a gentle but firm way.

Consistent monitoring, with love, of our internal affairs can be combined with inquisitiveness into our many delusions.

This gentle but consistent approach allows far-reaching traits to surface and be explored with grace and equanimity.

Be open to allowing the acceptance of positive outcomes in life.

No matter how progressed we think we are in overcoming distraction and illusion, there is going to be another conflict to show us still more delusions.

When in confusion about whether to address a situation in this way or in that, I find patience in knowing that deep within me is a longing that will give me a surprising notion for resolution, as long as I have the creativity to notice.

Be patient and be willing to change as your access to truth becomes clearer. As we wander through the Universe, inspiration will be there when we need it.

Recognize love, friendship, acceptance, support, warmth, kinship, and all positive thoughts, emotions, and feelings.

You have been loved completely. That is the basis of your longing. Undreamed of possibilities are surrounding you. Quiet the mind. Let them in.

Essay Index

Acknowledgments

My sincere appreciation to the Volcano Writer's Group for their inspiration of passion and creativity in writing. Special appreciation to Beatrix Sullivan.

To Sacred Dragon Publishing Services, a heartfelt thank you for bringing my book to the world, and a special thank you to Andi for her editing wizardry, artful wordsmithing, and good heart.

To every person I have encountered throughout my life and the *energy* we exchanged, I give thanks for showing me the complexities of diversity and compassion. Whether it was through love, antagonism, challenge, or the absurd, or whether it was in the moment or years later, each of these connections helped shape the person I am today.

I especially want to acknowledge and share my deepest gratitude for my children, who continue to be my greatest source of love and wonder.

Lastly, I want to acknowledge and honor all the mistakes I made in life as I wandered, sometimes blindly, along my Soul's path. Without the mistakes, I would not have known joy.

About the Author

Steven is a lifelong artist and spiritual seeker who has traversed a diverse landscape of experiences. From humble beginnings in inner-city Pittsburgh to serving in the Navy and meeting the challenges of raising five children, his life has been a tapestry of contrasts. He transitioned from the time-crunched world of truck driving to the precision of engineering and from the bustling city life to the tranquility of Hawaii. Born with an innate love of sailing, Steven raced yachts and later shared his love of sailing with children, teaching them to sail with a loving and understanding heart.

In each phase, he has found a unique way to infuse spirituality into his daily life, adding a deeper meaning to his journey. Steven's lifelong exploration of spiritual and religious meaning is evident in his unique approach to the metaphysical world. *The Third Part,* his personal interpretation of the spiritual realm and its accessibility, is a testament to his independent spirit. It is a guide for those like him who prefer to forge their own spiritual path rather than conform to traditional religious institutions.

Steven lives in the rainforests of Hawaii near an active volcano where he writes, paints, bakes, takes care of his garden and home, works as a substitute teacher, and attends weekly ecstatic dances. His poems and short stories have addressed history as well as novelty, the unexpected, and the truth. The walls of his house are covered with his murals and small paintings. Steven's approach to writing, cooking, art, and dance all come from a love of life, the willingness to take chances, and faith in the reality of intention.